United States Government Accountability Office

Report to Congressional Requesters

I0455426

July 2013

FOREIGN ASSISTANCE

U.S. Programs Involving the Palestine Investment Fund

July 2013

GAO Highlights

Highlights of GAO-13-537, a report to congressional requesters

FOREIGN ASSISTANCE

U.S. Programs Involving the Palestine Investment Fund

Why GAO Did This Study

According to the State Department (State), the U.S. government is one of the largest donors to the Palestinian Authority. According to State, the U.S. government provided about $3 billion in total bilateral assistance for fiscal years 2008 through 2012. PIF was established by Palestinian Authority presidential decree in 2002 and became operational in 2003 as an investment company aimed at strengthening the Palestinian economy through strategic investments.

GAO was asked to provide information on U.S. involvement with the Palestine Investment Fund. This report describes (1) the nature and scope of U.S. government involvement with PIF, and (2) OPIC's and USAID's processes for vetting PIF and other non-U.S entities and individuals participating in programs involving PIF and PIF-owned entities. GAO reviewed documents and interviewed officials from U.S. agencies, PIF, and implementing partners.

What GAO Recommends

This report does not contain any recommendations.

View GAO-13-537. For more information, contact David Gootnick at (202) 512-3149 or gootnickd@gao.gov.

What GAO Found

U.S. agencies and implementing partners participate in various programs with the Palestine Investment Fund (PIF) or PIF-owned entities that include home mortgage financing, loan guarantees, and educational initiatives. First, the Overseas Private Investment Corporation (OPIC) along with PIF and other entities have committed to lend $485 million to the Affordable Mortgage and Loan Company (AMAL) to support mortgages for low- and medium-income borrowers in the West Bank. OPIC has committed to lend about $313 million; PIF has committed about $72 million, and two banks account for the balance of the committed lending. However, as of April 2013, OPIC and PIF had not yet disbursed any funds. Second, OPIC and PIF are co-guarantors in a Loan Guarantee Facility (LGF) program in the West Bank, guaranteeing up to $110 million and $50 million in loans, respectively, to nine regional banks to support lending to small- and medium-sized enterprises. Third, USAID officials stated that, in 2009, USAID provided a U.S. implementing partner $2.1 million for technical assistance and training to enhance the lending practices of participating banks in support of the LGF. Finally, according to USAID, it provided about $1.3 million from 2010 to 2013 to three U.S. implementing partners to provide technical, in-kind, and scholarship assistance to the American International School in Gaza (AISG), which is owned by the Palestine Technology and Education Complex, a PIF-owned entity. According to USAID, its involvement with AISG ended in June 2013.

OPIC's and USAID's processes for vetting PIF and other non-U.S. entities and individuals in programs involving PIF and PIF-owned entities rely on various information sources. For the AMAL program, the two banks that issue mortgages are required under the AMAL agreements to vet potential borrowers for terrorist financing against such information sources as Treasury's Office of Foreign Asset Control Specially Designated Nationals and Blocked Persons List (OFAC) and the Compendium of United Nations Security Council Sanctions Lists; AMAL and OPIC are to conduct additional vetting. OPIC officials stated that OPIC has vetted PIF's board of directors and senior executives, the non-U.S. board members and shareholders of AMAL, and key officials of the banks against information sources such as the FBI Terrorist Screening Center database, OFAC list, and OPIC's Information Center databases. For the LGF program, OPIC said that, based on OPIC's procedures and the LGF agreements, it has vetted all the participating banks and has vetted key officials of each borrower and guarantor before loans are approved using information sources such as Treasury's Office of Terrorist Financing and Financial Crimes and FBI's Terrorist Screening Center databases. According to USAID officials, its process for vetting key participants of the Technical Assistance and Training program and the AISG program was based on documented vetting procedures for the West Bank and Gaza Mission. USAID officials said that all banks that participated in the LGF program that received training and technical assistance from USAID were subject to USAID's formal vetting process. USAID said it vetted information about AISG's owners and management against law enforcement and intelligence community systems accessed by USAID's Office of Security and through discussions with the U.S. Consulate General in Jerusalem, as applicable.

_____ **United States Government Accountability Office**

Contents

Figures

Abbreviations

AED	Academy for Educational Development (renamed FHI 360)
AISG	American International School in Gaza
AMAL	Affordable Mortgage and Loan Company
AMIDEAST	America-Mideast Educational and Training Services
CHF International	Cooperative Housing Foundation (renamed Global Communities)
ESAF	Expanded and Sustained Access to Financial Services
LGF	loan guarantee facility
MEII	Middle East Investment Initiative
OPIC	Overseas Private Investment Corporation
PIF	Palestine Investment Fund
PTEC	Palestine Technology and Education Complex
SAKAN	Palestinian Affordable Housing Association
SME	small- and medium-sized enterprises
State	Department of State
TAT	Technical Assistance and Training Program
USAID	U.S. Agency for International Development

July 25, 2013

The Honorable Nita M. Lowey
Ranking Member
Subcommittee on State, Foreign Operations, and Related Programs
Committee on Appropriations
House of Representatives

The Honorable Ted Deutch
House of Representatives

The Honorable Steve Israel
House of Representatives

The Palestine Investment Fund (PIF) was created by the Palestinian Authority to strengthen the Palestinian economy and assist with the economic development of the West Bank and Gaza. Both the Overseas Private Investment Corporation (OPIC) and U.S. Agency for International Development (USAID) are participating in programs involving PIF and a PIF-owned entity in the West Bank and Gaza. You asked us for information on the nature and extent of U.S. assistance for PIF and how U.S. agencies help ensure that U.S. assistance does not support terrorist activities.

This report describes (1) the nature and scope of U.S. government involvement with PIF, and (2) OPIC's and USAID's processes for vetting PIF and other non-U.S. entities and individuals participating in programs involving PIF and PIF-owned entities.[1]

To address these objectives, we reviewed and analyzed annual reports, U.S. antiterrorism policies, agency-specific vetting policies and procedures, and applicable program agreements obtained from PIF and relevant U.S. agencies and their implementing partners.[2] We also

---

[1]For purposes of this report, "vetting" refers to obtaining background or biographical information about an entity or individual or obtaining such information and checking it against relevant information sources to determine eligibility for the programs described in this report.

[2]U.S. agencies channel U.S. assistance through entities such as multilateral organizations, non-governmental organizations, and recipient country governments that serve as implementing partners.

interviewed officials of OPIC, USAID, the Departments of State (State) and Treasury, as well as various U.S. agencies' implementing partners. We also interviewed a high-level PIF official. We did not review PIF or its programs in which U.S. agencies are not participants. We described the vetting process represented to us by OPIC, USAID, and their implementing partners, based on agencies' applicable policies, procedures, and program agreements. We did not determine the extent to which OPIC and USAID implemented or complied with their vetting policies and procedures or assessed the effectiveness of OPIC's and USAID's vetting. See appendix I for a detailed discussion of our objectives, scope, and methodology.

We conducted this performance audit from October 2012 to July 2013 in accordance with generally accepted government auditing standards. Those standards require that we plan and perform the audit to obtain sufficient, appropriate evidence to provide a reasonable basis for our findings and conclusions based on our audit objectives. We believe that the evidence obtained provides a reasonable basis for our findings and conclusions based on our audit objectives.

Background

The West Bank and Gaza are comprised of about 2,400 square miles and have a combined population of 4.3 million people. The Palestinian Authority and Israel administer areas within the West Bank, and the Hamas-controlled de facto authorities operate in Gaza.

A negotiated two-state solution to the Israeli-Palestinian conflict is a core U.S. national security objective, according to State. The U.S. government's foreign assistance program in the West Bank and Gaza is designed to advance progress toward the two-state solution by helping the Palestinian Authority build the institutions of a future Palestinian state, creating an atmosphere that supports negotiations, and improving the everyday lives of Palestinians, thereby contributing to the overall stability and security of the region.

The U.S. government has provided assistance to the West Bank and Gaza both bilaterally and multilaterally for several decades. According to the State Department, the U.S. government is one of the largest donors to the Palestinian Authority. According to State and USAID, the U.S. government provided about $3 billion in bilateral assistance for fiscal years 2008 through 2012 to support education and social services, economic development, and humanitarian assistance, among other sectors. According to USAID, the U.S. government plans to provide $427 million in fiscal year 2013. USAID is the agency that is primarily responsible for implementing bilateral development and economic assistance, while State oversees annual contributions for multilateral programs. In support of the educational and financial sectors, USAID has provided awards to implementing partners to carry out programs and initiatives in the West Bank and Gaza. OPIC has supported the financial sector by providing loans and loan guarantees to eligible entities.

PIF was established by Palestinian Authority presidential decree in 2002 and became operational in 2003 as an investment company aimed at strengthening the Palestinian economy through strategic investments. As of 2012, the year of the most recent annual report available, PIF managed about $780 million in assets through multiple wholly owned subsidiaries, as well as minority ownership investments, with Palestinian investments accounting for 84 percent of its total investments. PIF is governed by a board of directors and a general assembly appointed by the Palestinian Authority President, and manages investments throughout a number of sectors, including real estate and hospitality, infrastructure, finance, capital markets, small-and-medium-sized enterprises (SMEs), and manufacturing. Appendix II provides a time line of key events in the development of PIF.

U.S. agencies must comply with certain restrictions under U.S. law when providing funds for Palestinian assistance programs, including restrictions reflecting U.S. policy to deny U.S. funds and other support to individuals or organizations that engage in or otherwise support terrorist activity. This policy is established in laws, executive orders, and regulations that, according to USAID and OPIC officials, provide the basis for USAID and OPIC terrorism vetting policies and procedures used to vet PIF and other entities and individuals associated with PIF-related programs in which USAID and OPIC are involved. Appendix III of this report outlines the legal framework for U.S. antiterrorism policy and describes applicable USAID and OPIC vetting policies and procedures.

U.S. Agencies Participate in Various Programs with PIF or PIF-owned Entities

Two U.S. agencies—OPIC and USAID—are involved in programs with PIF and a PIF-owned entity. OPIC participates in home mortgage financing and small business loan guarantee programs along with PIF. USAID provided technical assistance and training to benefit participating banks in the Loan Guarantee Facility (LGF) program[3] and has participated in educational programs at the American International School in Gaza, which is owned by PIF through a special purpose vehicle.[4]

OPIC, PIF, and Commercial Banks Are Co-Lenders to the Affordable Mortgage and Loan Program in the West Bank

OPIC, PIF, and local and regional commercial banks are co-lenders to the for-profit Affordable Mortgage and Loan Company (AMAL) in the West Bank, which is aimed at encouraging mortgage lending to low- and medium-income borrowers. AMAL was established in 2010, and OPIC officials told us that the purpose of the program is to purchase home mortgage loans from participating banks, as a means to reduce the banks' risk in mortgage lending. According to OPIC, as of April 2013, the two participating banks—the Cairo-Amman Bank and the Bank of Palestine—have agreed to issue mortgages under the AMAL program. OPIC officials told us that when fully operational, AMAL will purchase and refinance mortgages from the participating banks with combined financing from all of the co-lenders, including OPIC and PIF. AMAL will oversee and administer the mortgage financing, while the originating banks will continue to service the mortgages and interface with the borrowers. According to OPIC, as of April 2013, AMAL is partially operational and has originated and disbursed approximately four mortgages, all of which are directly funded by the participating banks. OPIC officials stated that OPIC and PIF have not yet financed any mortgage purchases under the AMAL program.

Under the AMAL Common Agreement, OPIC has committed to lend $313 million to AMAL (about 65 percent of the total debt commitment),[5] while

---

[3]According to USAID, it was not a loan guarantor under the LGF program and did not provide cash assistance to participating banks.

[4]A special purpose vehicle is a legal entity that a company creates to carry out some specific financial purpose or activity for the company that creates it. Special purpose vehicles can be used for purposes such as securitizing loans to help spread the credit and interest rate risk of their portfolios over a number of investors.

[5]According to OPIC, the International Finance Corporation—a member of the World Bank Group—has committed to provide a $72 million guarantee to OPIC's lending commitment to AMAL, reducing OPIC's principal at risk to $241 million.

PIF has committed to lend $72 million (about 15 percent of AMAL's total debt commitment). According to the Common Agreement, when the Cairo-Amman Bank and the Bank of Palestine cumulatively originate up to $10 million in eligible mortgage loans, the funding of the OPIC and PIF financial commitments to AMAL will take effect.[6] Figure 1 shows a graphical representation of the complex relationship of AMAL's financial structure and U.S. involvement in the program.

---

[6]According to OPIC officials, as of April 2013, the participating banks have issued four mortgage loans, totaling about $430,000.

GAO-13-537 Palestine Investment Fund

Figure 1: U.S. Involvement with the Affordable Mortgage and Loan Company and Complex Financial Structure

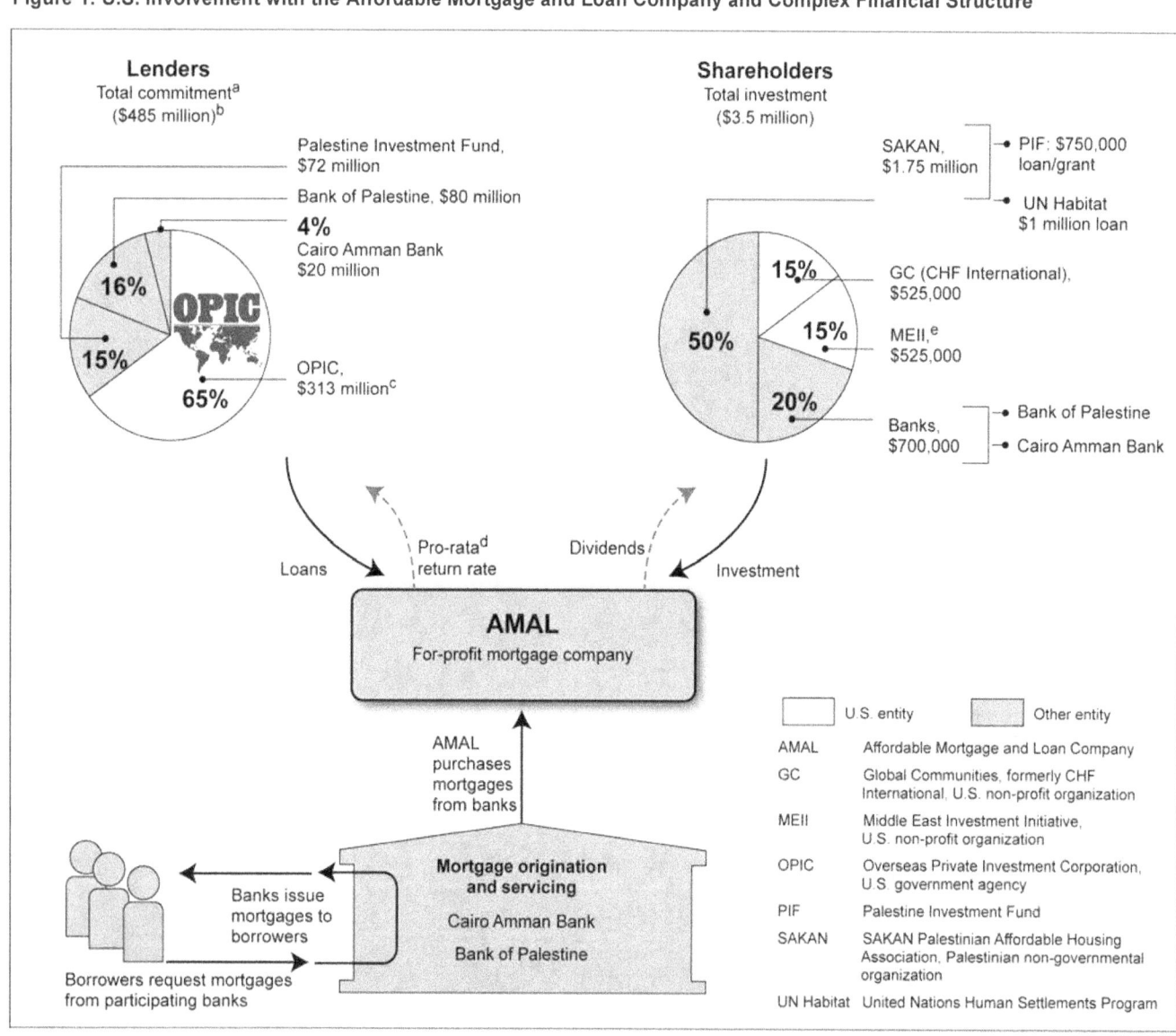

Source: GAO analysis of OPIC and AMAL data; OPIC (logo).

[a]The United Kingdom's Department for International Development has committed a first loss reserve to cover the first £13.33 million (about $20 million, based on the exchange rate as of July 10, 2013) in losses the lenders to AMAL may incur.

[b]According to OPIC, as of April 2013, no loan disbursements have been made by OPIC or PIF to AMAL. OPIC officials stated that OPIC and PIF's disbursements under their respective financial commitments will begin when the participating banks have amassed $10 million in qualifying mortgages to sell to AMAL.

°The International Finance Corporation has committed to provide a $72 million guarantee of OPIC's lending commitment to AMAL, reducing OPIC's principal at risk to $241 million.

ᵈPro-rata means the return rate is based on each lender's principal proportion at risk.

ᵉMEII manages its investment in AMAL through MEII Partners, LLC.

In the event of a default, the United Kingdom Department for International Development has committed £13.33 million (about $20 million, based on the exchange rate as of July 10, 2013) in first loss coverage to AMAL's co-lenders; and according to OPIC, additional losses will be incurred by all lenders on a pro-rata basis, determined by each co-lender's principal proportion at risk. Under the AMAL Shareholders Agreement, AMAL is owned by five shareholders that have provided a total investment of $3.5 million and, according to OPIC, will be paid dividends based on AMAL's performance. The Palestinian Affordable Housing Association (SAKAN), a Palestinian non-governmental organization, received assistance from PIF and the United Nations Human Settlements Program (UN Habitat) to fund its investment in AMAL. Under this agreement, SAKAN holds 50 percent of AMAL's shares, while two U.S. non-profit organizations—Global Communities (formerly CHF International) and the Middle East Investment Initiative (MEII), a non-profit U.S. entity created by the Aspen Institute [7]—account for 30 percent of AMAL's ownership, with the participating banks holding the remainder of AMAL's shares.[8]

OPIC and PIF Are Co-Guarantors to the Loan Guarantee Facility in the West Bank

In 2007, OPIC, along with PIF and MEII, launched a $160 million loan guarantee facility (LGF), which OPIC officials told us is aimed at encouraging commercial banks to provide loans to SMEs in the West Bank. According to the LGF Framework Agreement, participating banks receive assurance that OPIC and PIF will together cover 70 percent of each loan in the event of a default.

Under the LGF Framework Agreement, OPIC has committed $110 million to guarantee 48 percent of each eligible bank loan, through MEII, while PIF, as co-guarantor, has committed $50 million to guarantee 22 percent of each loan, in the event a borrower defaults on a LGF loan. According to OPIC officials, as of February 2013, OPIC has issued guarantees on

[7]The Aspen Institute is an educational and policy studies organization based in Washington, DC, with a mission to foster leadership based on enduring values and to provide a nonpartisan venue for dealing with critical issues.

[8]According to MEII, it manages its investment in AMAL through MEII Partners, LLC.

GAO-13-537 Palestine Investment Fund

about $85 million in LGF loans (about 77 percent of its total commitment) to MEII, which manages the LGF and serves as a coordinating agent between the loan guarantors and the banks. Figure 2 provides a detailed graphical depiction of the complexities of the U.S.'s involvement with the LGF program and a potential default scenario.

Figure 2: Complex Nature of U.S. Involvement with the Loan Guarantee Facility, and Potential Default Scenario

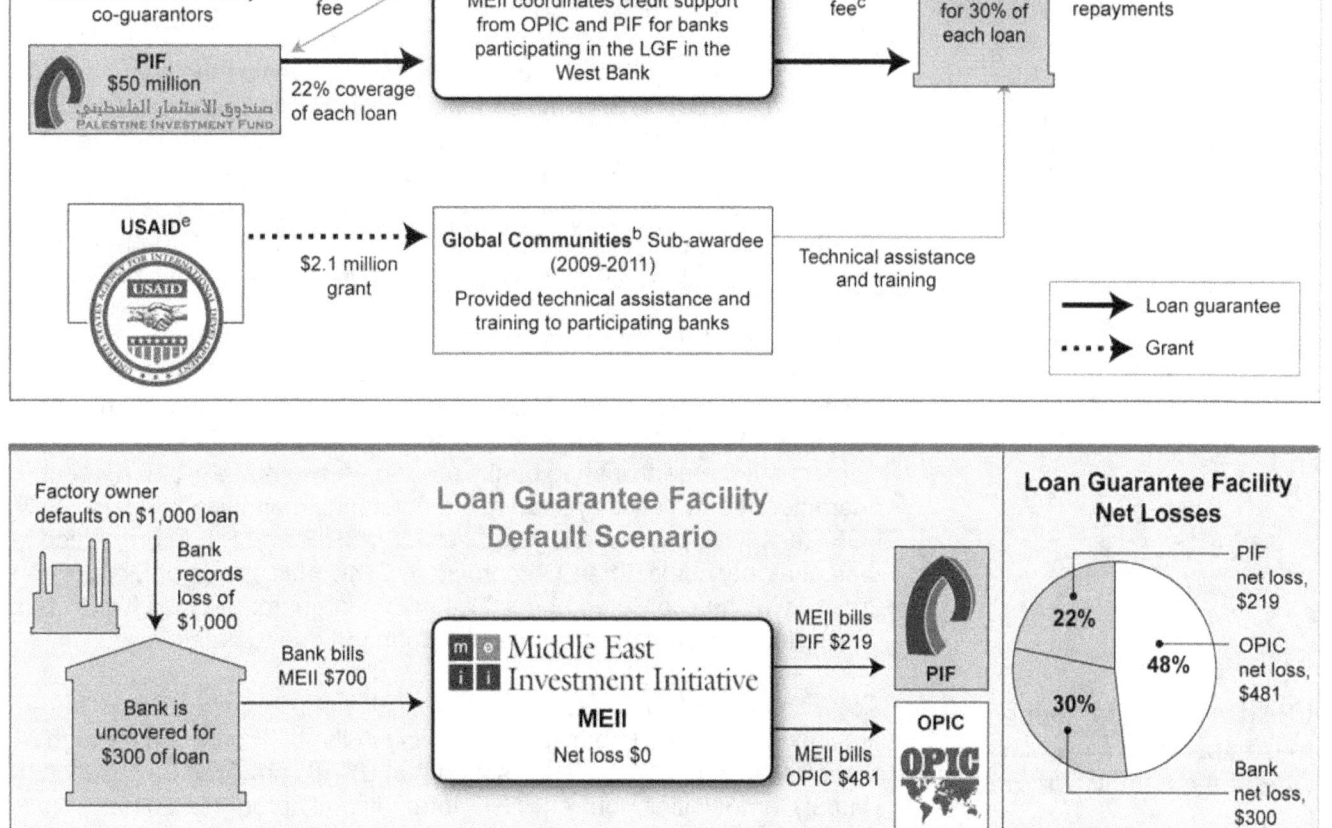

Source: GAO analysis of OPIC, PIF, and MEII data; OPIC, PIF, MEII, and Corel Graphics (logos).

aAccording OPIC officials, as of February 2013, OPIC has guaranteed $ 85,332,500 (77 percent of its total commitment) in LGF loans. According to OPIC, LGF management, subject to OPIC's approval, has until the end of fiscal year 2015 to allocate OPIC's remaining $24,667,500 (23 percent of OPIC's total commitment) to the participating banks.

bGlobal Communities, formerly CHF International, received this $2,093,354 sub-award as part of FHI 360's, formerly Academy for Educational Development (AED), 3-year, about $36.3 million USAID award for expanded and sustained access to financial services (ESAF) in the West Bank and Gaza.

cAccording to the LGF Guaranty Agreement, co-guarantors receive a 1.375 percent guarantee fee, divided on a pro-rata basis based on their guarantee percentages, which is applied to the outstanding principal amount of all LGF loans.

dAs of April 2013, nine commercial banks and one microfinance institution were participating in the LGF program.

eUSAID stated that it provided assistance to banks under the Technical Assistance and Training program to complement LGF, but was not a loan guarantor under the LGF program and did not provide cash assistance to participating banks.

Under the Guaranty Facility Agreement, MEII serves as the coordinating agent and, according to OPIC and MEII officials, only disburses OPIC funds in the event of a default by a borrower of an LGF loan. According to OPIC, as of February 2013, it has paid out about $1.2 million in default claims for LGF loans, while its share of outstanding loans in default was about $660,000 (48 percent of the total outstanding amount of about $1.4 million). PIF's share of outstanding loans in default was about $300,000 (22 percent), while the banks' share was about $410,000 (30 percent), according to OPIC. As shown in the lower panel of figure 2, the commercial bank that originates a loan is responsible for 30 percent of the defaulted loan amount. The remaining 70 percent is covered by OPIC (48 percent) and PIF (22 percent). Under the Guaranty Facility Agreement, the participating banks are required to pay a 1.375 percent guarantee fee, which is applied to the outstanding principal amount of all LGF loans, with payments divided between OPIC and PIF in proportion to their guaranty commitment. According to OPIC officials, as of March 2013, OPIC has collected about $1.4 million in guarantee fees, which has covered the amount the agency has expended due to defaults.

USAID Provided Support to Complement the Loan Guarantee Facility Program

According to USAID and Global Communities officials, USAID has provided assistance to banks participating in the LGF program through a grant that ended in 2011. They stated that USAID provided $2.1 million to Global Communities, formerly CHF International, through a prime awardee, for a 3-year program to provide technical assistance and training to banks participating in LGF to enhance these banks' lending practices.[9] According to USAID, although the Technical Assistance and Training program complemented the LGF program, it was an independent program with the goal of improving the capacity of Palestinian financial sector institutions.

USAID Has Funded Two Assistance Programs at the American International School in Gaza, a PIF-Owned Entity

Beginning in 2010, USAID provided assistance to the American International School in Gaza (AISG), a private school that offers a Western-style curriculum, as part of the agency's educational initiatives in the West Bank and Gaza. According to USAID and a PIF official, AISG is legally owned by the Palestine Technology and Education Complex (PTEC),[10] a PIF-owned entity. PTEC was described to us by a PIF official as a "special purpose vehicle" through which PIF owns AISG. According to the PIF official, AISG operates at a loss and PIF funds the school to close the school's deficit, as part of PIF's social corporate responsibility program. Over the past 6 academic years, PIF's funding of AISG has ranged from about $255,000 to about $465,000 annually.

According to USAID, it has granted awards to three implementing partners in support of AISG, providing an estimated $1.3 million in assistance from 2010 to 2013. These awards funded two projects providing need-based scholarships, technical assistance, supplies, and capacity building initiatives at AISG. According to USAID officials, USAID's primary AISG assistance program, originally implemented by the Democracy Council—a U.S. non-profit entity— was a 2 ½ -year, about $2 million award that focused on building the operational capacity,

---

[9]Global Communities, formerly CHF International, received this sub-award as part of a USAID award to FHI 360, formerly the Academy for Educational Development (AED). According to USAID, the award was for approximately a 3-year period for about $36.3 million to implement the Expanded and Sustained Access to Financial Services (ESAF) program in the West Bank and Gaza.

[10]According to a senior PIF official, PIF's ownership of PTEC is "indirect" with the Palestine Commercial Services Company, a wholly owned PIF subsidiary, holding 95 percent of PTEC's shares with the remaining 5 percent held by PIF. According to the PIF official, PTEC's board of directors is comprised of three members, all PIF officers. PTEC was established in 1999, prior to the establishment of PIF and, according to a PIF official, PTEC's ownership structure is a legacy from the time PTEC was established. According to this PIF official, a board of directors is required under Palestinian law and the board members have signing authority on behalf of PTEC. This official also told us that the PTEC board of directors has delegated signing authority for the PTEC bank account to AISG school management for daily operational matters.

management efficiency, and academic levels of AISG.[11] USAID officials stated that the bulk of the project funds were used for technical and in-kind assistance to AISG with no money directly transferred to the school; however, they stated that the Democracy Council provided 21 need-based scholarships ($63,000 total) for students to attend AISG, with funding deposited into AISG's bank account. USAID cancelled the Democracy Council award early because, according to USAID officials, the Democracy Council was unable to achieve programmatic goals and comply with the terms of the award. According to USAID officials, because USAID funds awards incrementally, about $1 million of the award had been funded and spent at the time of cancellation. After cancellation, USAID continued the need-based scholarship component of the award through the 2012-2013 academic year for 15 students ($45,000 total), implemented under the Mercy Corps' Palestinian Community Assistance Program. According to USAID, the scholarships will not be continued beyond the 2012-2013 academic year and the agency does not have any additional planned involvement at AISG.

According to USAID, in 2007, it provided a 5-year, $22.1 million award[12] to America-Mideast Educational and Training Services (AMIDEAST) to implement the Model Schools Network, an institutional capacity-building initiative focused on improving the quality of basic education, which, according to AMIDEAST officials, originally operated in the West Bank and expanded into Gaza in 2010. According to USAID and AMIDEAST officials, through the Model Schools Network award, from 2010 to 2012, AMIDEAST provided an estimated $323,000 to AISG through 127 need-based scholarships for students (about $220,000 total) and technical and in-kind assistance (estimated $103,000). USAID officials told us that the need-based scholarship component of the award, which expired in June 2012, was paid with USAID award funds by AMIDEAST to AISG's bank account. USAID officials also told us that the technical assistance component of this award, which also ended in June 2012, did not provide money directly to the school. According to USAID officials, in December 2012, USAID decided not to pursue further support for AISG through the Model Schools Network for the remainder of the award, which expired

---

[11]In its technical comments on a draft of this report, USAID stated that this project was entitled USAID-DC Educating for Peace.

[12]According to USAID officials, while this award was for $22.1 million, $21.1 million was obligated.

June 2013. Figure 3 depicts the complex structure of U.S. involvement with AISG.

Figure 3: Complex Structure of U.S. Involvement with the American International School in Gaza

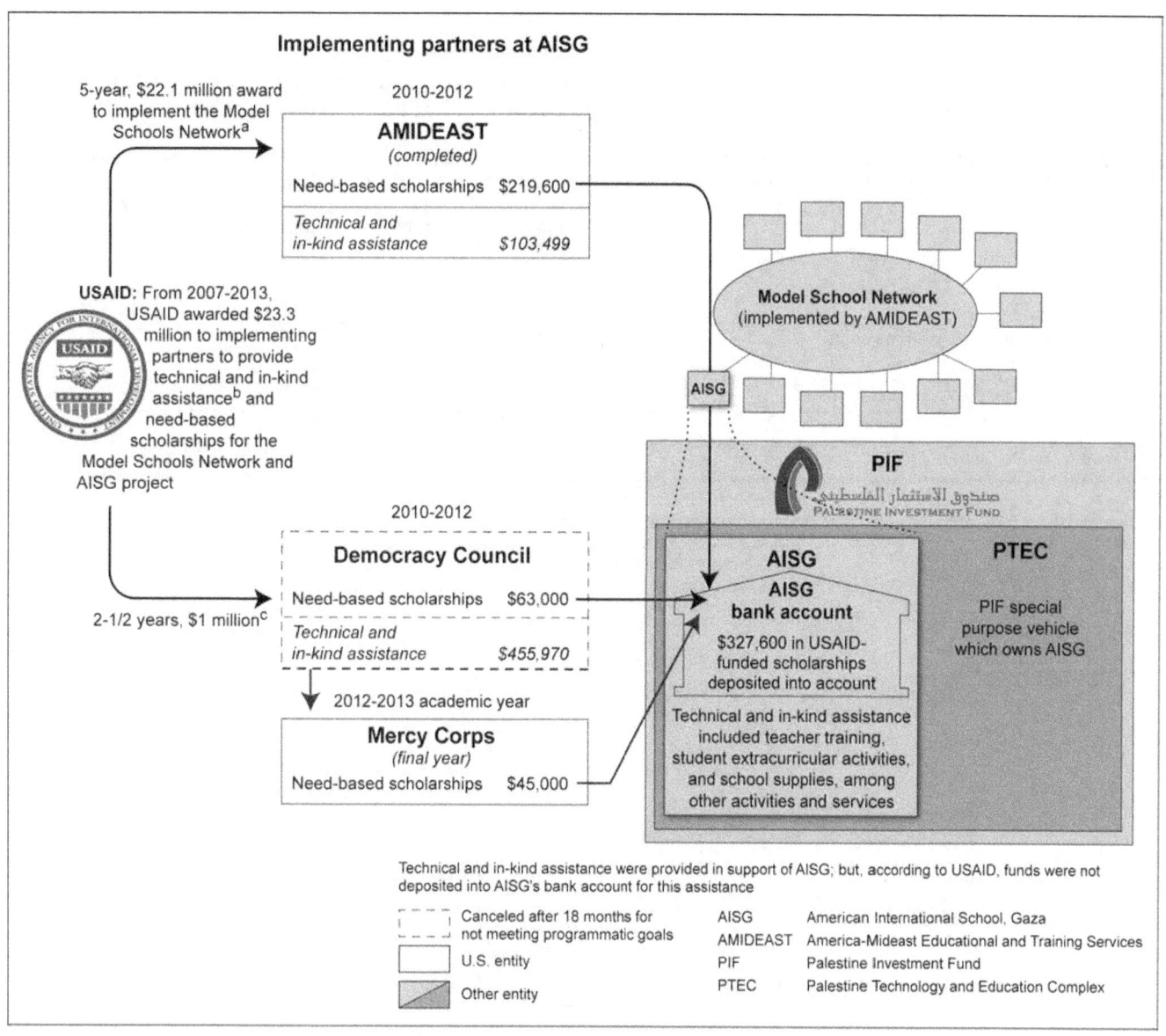

Source: GAO analysis of PIF and USAID data; Corel Graphics and PIF (logos).

[a]The Model Schools Network began operating in the West Bank in 2007 and in Gaza in 2010. In Gaza, in 2010, MSN worked with 12 private schools, 1 of which was AISG. At that time the MSN program was also comprised of 40 public and 17 private schools in the West Bank.

[b]In-kind assistance included teacher training, capacity building, and student extracurricular activities. Implementing partners provided these services to AISG.

[c]According to USAID, the original award was for $2 million over 2 ½ -years; however, the total costs for Democracy Council and Mercy Corps to implement this program were $1,003,512. This total includes $421,542 in administrative and other indirect costs incurred by Democracy Council and $18,000 in administrative and other indirect costs incurred by Mercy Corps.

According to USAID officials, USAID provided implementing partners in support of AISG an estimated total of about $1.3 million in assistance from 2010 to 2013. Table 1 shows the amount provided.

Table 1: USAID Implementing Partners' Assistance to the American International School in Gaza

Area of assistance	Implementing Partners' Assistance amounts		
	Democracy Council (2010-2011)	Mercy Corps (2012-2013 academic year)	AMIDEAST (2010-2012)
Technical Assistance (in kind, no cash provided to AISG)	$455,970	N/A	$103,499[a]
Scholarships (paid to AISG directly)	$63,000	$45,000	$219,600
Administrative and Other Indirect Costs	$421,542	$18,000	N/A
Total	**$940,512**	**$63,000**	**$323,099**

Source: GAO analysis of USAID data.

[a] AMIDEAST's estimated value for in-kind assistance to AISG, provided by USAID. Technical assistance information and administrative and other indirect costs for schools in the MSN are not recorded by individual school.

OPIC's and USAID's Processes for Vetting PIF or Entities and Individuals in Programs Involving PIF Rely on Various Information Sources

OPIC's and USAID's processes for vetting PIF, a PIF-owned entity, or other entities and individuals in the AMAL, LGF, and AISG assistance programs rely on various information sources, including information provided by their implementing partners.[13] Our description of the vetting processes and information sources is based on OPIC and USAID vetting policies and procedures; interviews with OPIC and USAID officials as well as officials of their implementing partners; and information in each program's agreements.[14]

OPIC and Other Relevant Entities' Processes for Vetting the AMAL and LGF Programs Rely on Various Information Sources

According to OPIC officials, OPIC's vetting of PIF and other non-U.S. entities and key individuals involved in the AMAL and LGF programs is based primarily on the agency's Character Risk Due Diligence policies and procedures and the applicable program's agreements.[15] The purpose of Character Risk Due Diligence is to uncover any derogatory information—including risks for terrorist financing and money laundering—about projects in which OPIC is involved, the project sponsors, investors, or key personnel. In performing due diligence, a project team is to make use of information sources that may include (1) OPIC's Information Center databases,[16] (2) the FBI's Terrorist Screening Center database[17] and Treasury's Financial Crimes Enforcement Network,[18] (3) the U.S. Embassy, any local counsel, and when required,

---

[13]U.S. agencies must comply with restrictions under U.S. law regarding assistance or support to terrorists when providing funds for Palestinian assistance programs. Appendix III of this report outlines the framework for U.S. antiterrorism policy and describes applicable USAID and OPIC vetting policies and procedures.

[14]We did not validate whether OPIC and USAID implemented or complied with their vetting policies and procedures.

[15]See app. III for details on OPIC's Character Risk Due Diligence procedures.

[16]OPIC's Information Center databases include more than 300 databases covering such lending concerns as creditworthiness, character risk, ties to senior government officials, international sanctions violations, and prior legal issues.

[17]The FBI Terrorist Screening Center database maintains the U.S. government's consolidated terrorist watchlist—a single database of identifying information about those known or reasonably suspected of being involved in terrorist activity.

[18]Treasury's Financial Crimes Enforcement Network mission is to safeguard the financial system from illicit use and combat money laundering and promote national security through the collection, analysis, and dissemination of financial intelligence and strategic use of financial authorities.

Outsourced Foreign Searches through the Information Center,[19] (4) the State Department Bureau of Intelligence and Research,[20] and (5) Office of Investment Policy,[21] with respect to derogatory information regarding social responsibility, corporate image, and environmental accountability.

Vetting Processes for the AMAL Program

The banks, AMAL, and OPIC conduct vetting to help ensure that there is no unacceptable derogatory information regarding non-U.S. entities and individuals participating in the AMAL program that might prevent OPIC support, according to OPIC.

Banks' Procedures for Vetting Borrowers and Guarantors

Under the AMAL agreements, when borrowers and guarantors[22] request loans from the Bank of Palestine and Cairo-Amman Bank, they are to provide specific information, such as their national identity card, passport, or similar identification to the banks, which are to conduct security and character vetting. Using this information, the Bank of Palestine and Cairo-Amman Bank are required to check borrowers and guarantors in accordance with specified internationally accepted Know-Your-Customer Check standards.[23] Specifically, the banks must verify at the time the

---

[19]According to OPIC, OPIC project teams can request Outsourced Foreign Searches when they determine that additional background information is needed on certain individuals or entities. OPIC maintains relationships with established and respected foreign providers of background checks, which undertake these searches when contracted by OPIC.

[20]State Department Bureau of Intelligence and Research provides value-added independent analysis of events to U.S. State Department policymakers; ensures that intelligence activities support foreign policy and national security purposes; and serves as the focal point in the State Department for ensuring policy review of sensitive counterintelligence and law enforcement activities around the world.

[21]OPIC's Office of Investment Policy works to ensure that OPIC-supported projects are environmentally and socially sustainable; respect human rights, including workers' rights; have no negative impact on the U.S. economy; and encourage positive host country development effects.

[22]Under the AMAL agreements, the banks are required to vet each mortgage obligor. A mortgage obligor is the mortgagor, each co-borrower, guarantor, and co-guarantor who are obligated under the mortgage loan documents related to the mortgage loan.

[23]The Know-Your-Customer Check refers to customer due diligence activities that financial institutions and other regulated companies must perform to ascertain relevant information from their customers for the purpose of doing business with them and to effectively monitor suspicious transactions and comply with requirements to report suspicious activity.

mortgage loan is approved that each borrower and guarantor does not appear on the Palestine Monetary Authority Central Bank Blacklist,[24] Treasury's Office of Foreign Asset Control Specially Designated Nationals and Blocked Persons List (OFAC's list), and the Compendium of United Nations Security Council Sanctions Lists. Under the AMAL mortgage origination guidelines, the banks must certify completion of satisfactory vetting before a mortgage application can be approved for a loan under the AMAL program.

AMAL's Procedures for Vetting and Auditing of Mortgage Loans

Under AMAL agreements, AMAL is to verify that the banks' origination criteria, including Know-Your-Customer Checks, were met for at least the first 100 mortgage loans to assess compliance with the origination guidelines. In addition, AMAL has the right to sample or audit subsequent mortgage loans.

OPIC's Vetting of AMAL Program Participants

According to OPIC, it vetted the participants in the AMAL program— including PIF's board of directors and senior executives, non-U.S. board members of AMAL, non-U.S. AMAL shareholders, and key individuals of the banks—against the OFAC list, the FBI Terrorist Screening Center database, and other relevant databases.[25] Also, officials of Global Communities, a U.S. NGO contracted by AMAL for vetting assistance, said that PIF and other co-lenders follow OPIC's lead in determining which loans are eligible for the program. OPIC officials said that OPIC has conducted extensive vetting of PIF, including its board of directors and senior executives through discussions with the U.S. Consulate General in Jerusalem, which represents the United States in Jerusalem, the West Bank, and the Gaza Strip.[26] In addition, OPIC officials said that OPIC vetted the board of directors, senior executives, and major

---

[24]According to OPIC, the Palestine Monetary Authority Central Bank Blacklist is used in the Palestinian banking community as a list of persons and institutions with character risk/due diligence issues identified by the Palestine Monetary Authority.

[25]According to OPIC, it did not vet the bank customers; the bank customers were vetted by the banks subject to audit by AMAL.

[26]According to OPIC, the initial vetting of PIF was done in connection with the LGF project presentation to OPIC's board in 2005.

GAO-13-537 Palestine Investment Fund

shareholders with greater than 5 percent ownership of the Bank of Palestine and Cairo-Amman Bank. OPIC stated that it has vetted both the Bank of Palestine and Cairo-Amman Bank through Treasury's Office of Terrorist Financing and Financial Crimes and discussed the banks with the Palestine Monetary Authority, clearing the banks before OPIC entered into an agreement with them. Further, OPIC stated it has vetted the non-U.S. board members of AMAL, as well as AMAL shareholders, including the Palestinian Affordable Housing Association. Individual borrowers who have applied for loans should have been vetted by the banks subject to AMAL's origination guidelines, according to OPIC.

Vetting Processes for the LGF Program

The private banks and microfinance institutions (lenders), the coordinating agent (MEII), and OPIC conduct vetting to help ensure that there is no unacceptable derogatory information regarding entities and individuals participating in the LGF program that might prevent OPIC support, according to OPIC.

Private Banks' and Microfinance Institutions' Procedures for Vetting LGF Borrowers

Under the LGF Guaranty Facility agreements, prior to concluding loan agreements with SMEs, the LGF participating banks and microfinance institutions are to check the SMEs for potential terrorist connections against OFAC and the Compendium of United Nations Security Council Sanctions Lists and provide the vetting results to MEII. The agreements state that if a borrower is found to be on a screening list, the guarantee would not be approved; and if a borrower is found to be on a screening list after the guarantee has been allowed, the guarantee would no longer be in effect.

MEII's Procedures for Vetting LGF Borrowers and Lenders

As the coordinating agent for the LGF program, MEII is to vet all borrowers and lenders. MEII contracted with Global Communities to assist in reviewing loan applications and vetting the participants. Global Communities officials informed us that they checked the borrowers against the OFAC list to help ensure that borrowers were not blocked by Treasury's sanctions. According to OPIC, MEII took over this function directly in June 2010.

Based on the LGF operational manual, once a lender has indicated interest in participating in the LGF program, MEII is to confirm whether the lender is licensed to operate in the West Bank and Gaza under the

Palestine Monetary Authority and whether it meets the minimum requirement of a 51 percent private sector ownership of the lending institution. MEII is to obtain a written affirmation from the authority that the lender is in good standing with the authority, has government consent to operate, and complies with best banking practices, corrupt practices laws, and other standards.

MEII is to collect the necessary information from the lender to begin the U.S. government security and character vetting process, which includes vetting the lender as an institution, vetting all owners having more than 5 percent ownership, and vetting executive management. MEII is then to present the lender nomination proposal to OPIC and PIF officials who, according to OPIC, approve or reject the participation of the lenders.

According to OPIC officials and as provided in the LGF guaranty facility agreement, MEII is to provide the vetting results on the borrowers and lenders with other identifying information to OPIC. In addition, for all loans less than $500,000, MEII makes the loan decision based on credit eligibility requirements and subject to OPIC's ultimate decision pertaining to security and character vetting.[27]

OPIC's Vetting of LGF Borrowers, Lenders, and Guarantors

According to OPIC, it vets participants (lenders, borrowers, and guarantors) under the LGF program. OPIC said it provides information about each proposed participating bank to Treasury's Office of Terrorist Financing and Financial Crimes and inquires whether there is any unacceptable derogatory information in Treasury's databases that might prevent OPIC from supporting a particular lender. OPIC said that it has vetted and cleared all nine participating banks in the LGF program.[28]

According to OPIC, for all loans, regardless of size, when an LGF participating bank submits loan proposals to LGF management, it checks the names and identification information on individual owners, directors, and senior executive management of each borrower and guarantor

---

[27]OPIC officials told us that MEII has denied loan applications for credit policy reasons and based on its checks of the OFAC list, of which OPIC would not be informed.

[28]In commenting on the draft of this report, OPIC told us that one bank was recently refused participation in the LGF program due to concerns raised by the FBI's Terrorist Screening Center.

through the FBI's Terrorist Screening Center database before loans are approved. According to OPIC, from a credit standpoint, in cases where borrowers were seeking loans greater than $500,000, or if loans are provided to companies in Gaza, the loan application is sent to the three-person decisional committee representatives (from OPIC, MEII, and PIF). The officials stated that the loan is approved only if the decisional committee unanimously agrees, which means that any committee representative can veto a loan for any reason. However, OPIC stated that it ultimately approves each loan with regard to character vetting, and that it has denied loans proposed by LGF management when the borrower did not pass the Terrorist Screening Center database review.

In vetting PIF as a co-guarantor, OPIC stated that it also checked individual directors and senior executive management of PIF through the FBI's Terrorist Screening Center database. OPIC officials said that it also performed Character Risk Due Diligence through its own Information Center, consulted with the U.S. Consulate General in Jerusalem and the State Department, and had discussions with officials of the Palestinian Authority and Israeli Ministry of Defense. OPIC and MEII officials said that PIF would recuse itself if any of its subsidiaries applies for a loan, and that PIF does not have control over the lenders.

Further, OPIC said it checks information relating to the banks and microfinance institutions against other databases through OPIC Information Center databases (including the Compendium of United Nations Security Council Sanctions Lists and "Do Not Pay" list,[29] as applicable), as well as with the U.S. Consulate General in Jerusalem and other sources.

Treasury officials also informed us that, based on OPIC's request, Treasury has vetted PIF for the two projects PIF is involved in with OPIC. In addition, Treasury officials told us that its policy office made inquiries regarding how PIF's money is managed to help ensure it is not directly or indirectly being funneled to terrorists or terrorist organizations. According to Treasury officials, in both instances, Treasury did not find any derogatory information on PIF or any linkage to terrorist financing.

---

[29]The Do Not Pay list is a list of multiple data sources compiled by the U.S. government to help prevent, reduce, and stop improper payments from being made and to identify and mitigate fraud, waste, and abuse in programs administered and/or funded by the federal government.

GAO-13-537 Palestine Investment Fund

USAID's Process for Vetting the Technical Assistance and Training and AISG Programs Was Based on Its Mission Order 21 and Relied on Various Information Sources

According to USAID officials, USAID's process for vetting key participants of the Technical Assistance and Training program for Palestinian banks and the AISG program was based on the U.S. Mission to the West Bank and Gaza's Mission Order 21. Mission Order 21 establishes USAID's policies and procedures to help ensure that its assistance does not inadvertently provide support to entities or individuals associated with terrorism, including guidance on vetting and antiterrorism certification by USAID awardees.[30]

USAID's Vetting of Banks Participating in Technical Assistance and Training

USAID stated that as part of USAID's broader program to support Palestinian financial institutions, Global Communities, a U.S. sub-awardee, provided technical assistance and training to senior staff of participating banks in the LGF program, for which OPIC and PIF are co-guarantors. Based on Mission Order 21, if vetting was required, Global Communities was to obtain information on the banks and microfinance institutions' key individuals before they participate in training and provide the information to USAID.[31] According to USAID, USAID's Vetting Center in Washington, D.C. would check the names of key individuals through law enforcement and intelligence community systems accessed by USAID's Office of Security. In addition, USAID stated that for sub-grants and certain in-kind assistance, such as technical assistance, USAID submits the information to the U.S. Consulate General in Jerusalem for additional review. According to USAID, each of the banks participating in the Technical Assistance and Training program was subject to USAID's formal vetting procedures.

USAID's Vetting for the AISG Program

According to USAID, Mission Order 21 vetting procedures also apply to vetting for the AISG program. As described previously, AMIDEAST and Democracy Council were U.S. implementing partners through whom USAID implemented scholarships and in-kind assistance at AISG (a non-U.S. entity).[32]

---

[30]See app. III for details on USAID's Mission Order 21.

[31]USAID officials told us that AED/FHI 360, the prime awardee (implementing partner), is responsible for providing USAID with the names of key individuals and organizations that require vetting.

[32]According to USAID, although Mercy Corp later became a USAID implementing partner for AISG, Mercy Corp was not required to play any role in the vetting process because AISG had already been vetted less than 12 months before Mercy Corps became involved.

GAO-13-537 Palestine Investment Fund

Implementing Partners' Collection of Information Provided to USAID for Vetting

AMIDEAST and Democracy Council officials said that they provided information about AISG owners and key personnel to USAID, as required by the terms of their contracts. Specifically, AMIDEAST and Democracy Council officials said they provided information such as name, date and place of birth, occupation, and copies of passport or national identification cards for AISG owners and employees to USAID for vetting of AISG.

USAID's Vetting of Relevant Entities and Key Individuals in Connection with AISG

According to USAID and based on Mission Order 21, it vetted key individuals of PTEC, such as members of the board of directors, as well as AISG's management, such as the principal and vice-principal of the school, against law enforcement and intelligence community systems accessed by USAID's Office of Security and through discussions with U.S. Consulate General in Jerusalem, as applicable. USAID officials stated that it was not necessary to vet PIF, the parent company of PTEC, because PTEC is legally responsible for AISG.[33] USAID stated that the students who received scholarships and their parents were not vetted, consistent with Mission Order 21, because the students, who were the beneficiaries, were under the age of 16.

Agency and Third Party Comments and Our Evaluation

We provided a draft of this report to OPIC and USAID for their review and comment. OPIC and USAID provided technical comments, which we incorporated in this report as appropriate. We also provided portions of a draft of this report to PIF for review. PIF provided technical comments, which we incorporated as appropriate.

---

[33]Under USAID's Mission Order 21, USAID's Vetting Center in Washington, D.C., is to check the names of key individuals through law enforcement and intelligence community systems accessed by USAID's Office of Security and submit the information to the U.S. Consulate General in Jerusalem for additional review, as applicable.

As agreed with your offices, unless you publicly announce the contents of this report earlier, we plan no further distribution of this report until 30 days from the report date. At that time, we will send copies of this report to interested congressional committees, the Secretary of State, the Administrator of USAID, the President and Chief Executive Officer of the Overseas Private Investment Corporation, the appropriate congressional committees and other interested parties. In addition, the report will be available at no charge on the GAO website at http://www.gao.gov.

If you or your staff have any questions about this report, please contact me at (202) 512-3149 or gootnickd@gao.gov. Contact points for our Office of Congressional Relations and Public Affairs may be found on the last page of this report. GAO staff who made major contributions to this report are listed in appendix VI.

David Gootnick
Director, International Affairs and Trade

Appendix I: Objectives, Scope, and Methodology

Our objectives were to describe (1) the nature and scope of U.S. government involvement with the Palestine Investment Fund (PIF), and (2) OPIC's and USAID's processes for vetting PIF and other non-U.S. entities and individuals participating in programs involving PIF and PIF-owned entities.

To address our first objective, we reviewed and analyzed program agreements, annual reports, and other documents from OPIC, USAID, PIF, and OPIC's and USAID's implementing partners (AMIDEAST, CHF International/Global Communities, Democracy Council, Middle East Investment Initiative (MEII), and Mercy Corp). To describe the Affordable Mortgage and Loan (AMAL) and the Loan Guarantee Facility (LGF) programs in which OPIC is involved with PIF, we reviewed various documents, including the AMAL Common Agreement, AMAL's Mortgage Loan Origination and Purchase Agreement, OPIC's press release regarding its involvement with PIF in the AMAL program, PIF's description of the AMAL program, AMAL organization structure, the LGF Guaranty Facility Agreement, OPIC's signed LGF agreement, LGF Operational Manual, LGF organizational structure, as well as various documents containing responses to our questions from OPIC. To describe USAID's Technical Assistance and Training (TAT) and the American International School in Gaza (AISG) programs in which USAID is involved with a PIF-owned entity, we reviewed CHF International/Global Communities LGF-TAT quarterly, annual, and final reports for 2009-2011, USAID's West Bank/Gaza fact sheet on the Expanded and Sustained Access to Financial Services program (ESAF) under which USAID provides TAT, USAID's AISG project fact sheet, USAID's fact sheet on the Model School Network, Democracy Council's brochure on AISG, the AMIDEAST Model School Network Final Report, as well as various documents containing responses to our questions from USAID. We interviewed USAID officials about funds spent in support of programs at AISG and determined that the data were sufficiently reliable for our purposes. Further, we reviewed PIF's 2006 to 2012 annual reports to determine the involvement of U.S. agencies with PIF.

To address our second objective, we reviewed U.S. government-wide antiterrorism laws, executive orders, and regulations that provide the basis for USAID's and OPIC's terrorism policies and procedures for vetting PIF and other entities and individuals participating in programs involving PIF. (Appendix III provides the general legal framework for the U.S. antiterrorism policy and OPIC's and USAID's terrorist vetting policies and procedures.) For the AMAL and LGF programs in which OPIC is involved, we reviewed OPIC's Character Risk Due Diligence Policies and

Procedures, the AMAL program's common agreement, AMAL's Fixed
Rate Financing and Floating Rate Financing Agreements, AMAL
Shareholders Agreements, excerpts from the LGF Operational Manual,
and the LGF agreements. For the USAID TAT and AISG programs, we
reviewed CHF International/Global Communities' LGF-TAT quarterly,
annual, and final reports for 2009 to 2011, as well as various documents
containing responses to our questions from USAID. In addition, we
reviewed USAID's Mission Order No. 21, which establishes USAID's
vetting policies and procedures for its programs in the West Bank and
Gaza. We also reviewed Treasury's Licensure No. 7, which allows U.S.
entities to engage with Palestinian entities in the West Bank and Gaza.
Further, we reviewed prior GAO reports that discuss USAID's vetting
procedures for programs in which it is involved in the West Bank and
Gaza.[1] We described the information sources represented to us as being
used by OPIC, USAID, and other entities to vet PIF and program
recipients; however, we did not determine the extent to which OPIC and
USAID implemented or complied with their vetting policies and
procedures or assessed the effectiveness of OPIC's and USAID's vetting
because it is beyond the scope of this review. In addition, we did not
travel to the region to assess these programs or the agencies' vetting
procedures.

For both objectives, we interviewed officials from OPIC, State, Treasury,
USAID, PIF, CHF International/Global Communities, Middle East
Investment Initiative, AMIDEAST, and Democracy Council and received
written responses to our questions from Mercy Corps.

We conducted this performance audit from October 2012 to July 2013 in
accordance with generally accepted government auditing standards.
Those standards require that we plan and perform the audit to obtain
sufficient, appropriate evidence to provide a reasonable basis for our
findings and conclusions based on our audit objectives. We believe that
the evidence obtained provides a reasonable basis for our findings and
conclusions based on our audit objectives.

---

[1]GAO, *Foreign Assistance: U.S. Assistance to the West Bank and Gaza for Fiscal Years
2010 and 2011*, GAO-12-817R (Washington, D.C.: July 13, 2012); *Foreign Assistance:
Measures to Prevent Inadvertent Payments to Terrorists under Palestinian Aid Programs
Have Been Strengthened, but Some Weaknesses Remain*, GAO-09-622 (Washington,
D.C.: May 19, 2009); *Foreign Assistance: Recent Improvements Made, but USAID Should
Do More to Help Ensure Aid Is Not Provided for Terrorist Activities in West Bank and
Gaza*, GAO-06-1062R (Washington, D.C.: Sept. 29, 2006).

Appendix II: Time Line of Key Events in the Development of the Palestine Investment Fund

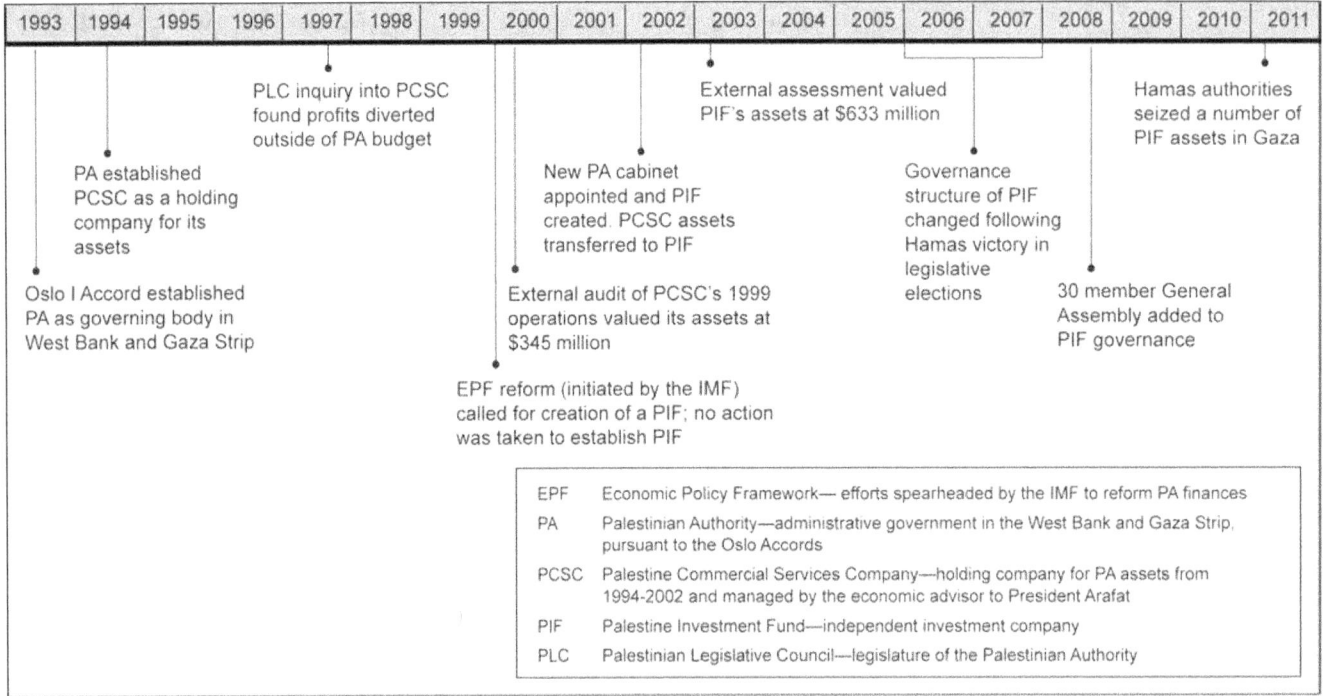

Source: GAO analysis of PIF, IMF, and World Bank information.

1993-1994: The Palestinian Authority Granted Control over Parts of the West Bank and Gaza. The government of Israel and the Palestine Liberation Organization signed the Oslo Peace Accords,[1] which called for the withdrawal of Israeli forces from parts of the West Bank and Gaza and affirmed the Palestinian right to self-government within those areas, under the Palestinian Authority. The Palestinian Authority was established in May 1994 to begin assuming self-governing responsibilities in the West Bank and Gaza Strip.

1994: PCSC, Forerunner of the Palestine Investment Fund (PIF), Established as a Holding Company. The Palestinian Authority began acquiring shareholdings in a number of companies across various sectors

---

[1]Oslo I Accords (Declaration of Principles on Interim Self-Government Arrangements), September 1993.

of the economy. According to a report by the World Bank,[2] these commercial undertakings were placed under the umbrella of a holding company, the Palestine Commercial Services Company (PCSC), managed by the economic advisor to the Palestinian Authority's then-president, Yasser Arafat. According to the World Bank Report, the PCSC had full equity ownership of the Cement Company, which held an exclusive contract for the import of cement from Israel. In addition, the report stated that PCSC had partnerships with private investors in numerous businesses, including hotels, casinos, cigarettes, telecoms, real estate, flour milling, and other sectors.

1997: Inquiry Finds PCSC Profits Diverted Outside of Palestinian Authority Budget. According to the World Bank report, following a public inquiry, the Palestinian Legislative Council found that PCSC was not monitored by the external audit body of the Palestinian Authority, known as the General Audit Institute, and that PCSC generated significant profits, which were diverted outside of the Palestinian Authority budget. Additionally, the report stated that the finances of the PCSC were not released to Palestinian Legislative Council members or the public.

2000: Initiative Calls for PIF Creation. The International Monetary Fund (IMF) and President Arafat initiated the Economic Policy Framework reform which, among other reforms, called for the creation of a Palestine Investment Fund, although no action was taken to establish such a fund at that time. According to a report by the IMF,[3] the Economic Policy Framework initiative resulted in two achievements: the consolidation of excise tax revenue within the Minister of Finance's office, and the auditing of the assets of the PCSC.

2000: External Audit Values PCSC's Asset at $345 million. An external audit of PCSC's 1999 operations found that the PCSC had net profits of $77 million and assets valued at $345 million. In addition to this audit, an IMF report found that many of PCSC's commercial operations were funded from diverted tax revenue. These commercial activities generated profits which, according to the IMF report, were also being diverted away

---

[2]The World Bank, *West Bank and Gaza: Improving Governance and Reducing Corruption*, Report number 61701-GZ (2011).

[3]International Monetary Fund, *West Bank and Gaza: Economic Performance and Reform under Conflict Conditions* (September 2003).

from the Palestinian Authority budget. Because PCSC did not publish balance sheets or annuals reports, the IMF reported that it was difficult to determine PCSC's profits between 1995 and 2000; however, the IMF estimated that about $300 million in profits from PCSC were channeled outside of the Palestinian Authority budget from 1995 to 2000.

2002 (June): Reform Plan Prepared. A new Palestinian Authority cabinet was appointed and a ministerial committee prepared a 100-day reform plan, which, according to an IMF report, began addressing revenue consolidation, budget reform, and monopolies, among other reforms.

2002 (October): PIF Formally Established. According to the World Bank report, as part of broader reforms the Palestinian Authority was undertaking under the 100-day plan, PIF was formally established by presidential decree, to consolidate all Palestinian Authority commercial activities and asset ownership. According to the report, it became illegal for the Palestinian Authority to conduct any commercial activity or hold any assets outside of PIF.

- According to a PIF official, the President appointed a board of directors, which included the Minister of National Economy and was chaired by the Minister of Finance.
- The report noted that the board of directors ordered a full valuation and transparency assessment of Palestinian Authority assets— previously held under PCSC—to be transferred to PIF.

2003: External Assessment Values PIF Assets at $633 million. The Democracy Council and Standard and Poor's published the valuation and transparency assessment of Palestinian Authority assets, as ordered by the board of directors.

- As of January 1, 2003, PIF assets were valued at $633 million, including 67 commercial entities and liquid assets.

2006-2007: PIF Governance Structure Changed Following Hamas Legislative Election Victory. According to PIF and U.S. officials, following the Hamas victory in the Palestinian legislative elections, President Abbas initiated major changes in the governance structure of PIF. According to a PIF official, the changes to the governance structure were initiated to insulate PIF's assets from Hamas interference. By Presidential decree, both the Minister of National Economy and the Minister of Finance were removed from the board and replaced by external appointees.

2008: President Appointed 30-member General Assembly. According to its annual report, PIF added a 30-member general assembly to its governance structure to provide strategic guidance to the board of directors, with the Palestinian Authority President appointing each assembly member to serve a 3-year term. According to a PIF official, this change was made in accordance with existing Palestinian corporate law and to enhance accountability, transparency, and good governance.

2011: Hamas Seized PIF Assets in Gaza. Hamas seized a number of PIF assets in Gaza, including PIF's branch office, a commercial building, and a juice factory. Following the seizure of assets, PIF officials released a statement denouncing the seizures as illegal and in violation of Palestinian law. A PIF official estimated the value of these assets at around $10 million, which PIF had to write off. According to this official, as of February 2013, PIF's only remaining asset in Gaza is vacant land, valued at about $5 million. The official also told us that PIF has no control over or access to the vacant land, which Hamas has publicly stated it has seized. However, the official noted that PIF continues to keep the land on its books because Hamas has not taken physical control of the land.

2013 (June): PIF currently governed by Board of Directors and Generally Assembly. According to PIF's audited financial statements and a PIF official, PIF is governed by a board of directors and a general assembly, both appointed by the Palestinian Authority President. The board of directors is comprised of 11 members responsible for setting and overseeing PIF's goals and objectives, while the general assembly, comprised of 30 members, provides strategic guidance to the board. According to PIF's publicly available annual financial statements, Ernst and Young was PIF's external auditor from 2006 to 2012. According to a PIF official, internal auditing functions at PIF are performed by Deloitte, to help ensure there are adequate internal controls and that management complies with the law and standards governing administrative and investment operations. This official also noted that PIF is audited by the Palestinian State Audit and Administrative Control Bureau.

Appendix III: Legal Framework for Terrorist Vetting by USAID and OPIC

U.S. agencies must comply with restrictions under U.S. law when providing funds for Palestinian assistance programs, including restrictions reflecting U.S. policy to deny U.S. funds and other support to individuals or organizations that engage in or otherwise support terrorist activity. This policy is established in laws, executive orders, and regulations that provide the basis for USAID and OPIC terrorism vetting policies and procedures used to vet PIF and other entities and individuals associated with PIF-related programs in which USAID and OPIC are involved.[1]

Government-Wide Antiterrorism Laws and Executive Orders

Various federal laws and executive orders dealing with terrorism allow the blocking or "freezing" of targeted assets located in the United States or under the control of a U.S. person outside of the United States. The International Emergency Economic Powers Act (IEEPA) (50 USC §§ 1701-1706) grants the president authority in times of emergency to block assets in the United States in which any foreign nation or national has an interest. Executive Order 12947 (Jan. 23, 1995, amended Aug. 20, 1998), issued pursuant to the IEEPA, declared an emergency with respect to "grave acts of terrorism committed by foreign terrorists that disrupt the Middle East peace process," and blocked all property subject to U.S. jurisdiction in which there is any interest of certain Middle East terrorist organizations included in an annex to that executive order.

The Antiterrorism and Effective Death Penalty Act of 1996 (the Antiterrorism Act) contains several relevant provisions. Section 302 of the Antiterrorism Act (18 USC § 2339A) makes it a criminal offense to, among other things, provide material support or resources to or conceal or disguise material support or resources with knowledge that such support or resources are to be used in the commission of a terrorist act. Section 303 of the Antiterrorism Act (18 USC § 2339B) makes it a criminal offense to provide material support or resources to such foreign organizations and requires financial institutions to block all funds in which foreign terrorists organizations or their agents have an interest. Under 8 USC § 1189, the Secretary of State is authorized to designate organizations as "foreign terrorist organizations" for purposes of Section 303 of the Antiterrorism Act. Section 321 of the Antiterrorism Act (18 USC § 2332d) makes it a criminal offense for U.S. persons, except as provided in regulations

---

[1]The laws, executive orders, and regulations referred to in this appendix are not intended to be exhaustive of all U.S. laws, executive orders, and regulations pertaining to antiterrorism.

issued by the Secretary of the Treasury in consultation with the Secretary of State and the Attorney General, to engage in financial transactions with the governments of countries designated under section 6(j) of the Export Administration Act of 1979 (50 USC App. § 2405) as supporting international terrorism.

The USA Patriot Act broadened the president's authority under the IEEPA by allowing the blocking of assets during the pendency of an investigation. Executive Order 13224 (Sept. 23, 2001), was issued pursuant to the IEEPA and the USA Patriot Act. This executive order prohibits all U.S. persons from engaging in any kind of transactions with persons, groups, or entities, or their supporters or associates, who commit, threaten to commit, or support terrorism and authorizes the Department of the Treasury to block all U.S. assets of certain individuals and entities listed in the executive order as "Specially Designated Global Terrorists" (SDGTs) and to list additional SDGTs.

In addition, since fiscal year 2003, annual foreign operations appropriations laws have included provisions requiring the Secretary of State, prior to obligation of Economic Support Funds (ESF) for assistance for the West Bank and Gaza, to take "appropriate steps to ensure that assistance is not provided to or through any individual, private or government entity, or education institution, that the Secretary knows or has reason to believe advocates, plans, sponsors, engages in, or has engaged in, terrorist activity." Since fiscal year 2005, annual foreign operations appropriations laws have also included provisions prohibiting provision of any funds appropriated under those laws for purposes of recognizing or otherwise honoring individuals who commit or have committed terrorist acts.[2]

Government-Wide Implementing Regulations

The Department of the Treasury's Office of Foreign Asset Control (OFAC) administers various U.S. sanctions programs, including the terrorism sanctions programs in 31 CFR Parts 595, 596 and 597 which implement

---

[2] See, Consolidated Appropriations Resolution, 2003, Pub. L. No. 108-7, § 568(b), Feb. 20, 2003, and Consolidated Appropriations Act, 2005, Pub. L. No. 108-447, Div. D, Title V, § 559(c), Dec. 8, 2004. See also, for example, Consolidated Appropriations Act, 2012, Pub. L. No.112-74, § 7039(b) and (c), Dec. 23, 2011, for an example of legislation containing both types of provisions. Similar provisions were included in the Palestinian Anti-Terrorism Act of 2006, Pub. L. No. 109-446, § 3(b)(2) and (3), Dec. 21, 2006, extending the requirements through fiscal years 2007 and 2008.

the above-cited laws and executive orders government-wide. The
Terrorism Sanctions Regulations at 31 CFR Part 595, which implement
Executive Order 12947, were issued pursuant to the IEEPA. The
Terrorism List Governments Sanctions Regulations at 31 CFR Part 596
implement section 321 of the Antiterrorism Act. The Foreign Terrorism
Organizations Sanctions Regulations at 31 CFR Part 597 implement
sections 302 and 303 of the Antiterrorism Act and 8 USC § 1189.[3]

OFAC licenses[4] have allowed in certain instances for USAID and its
grantees and contractors to engage in transactions with the Palestinian
Authority and related entities, including PIF, in order to conduct financial
transactions and other activities otherwise prohibited by the sanctions
programs in 31 CFR Parts 595, 596, and 597. OFAC has issued a series
of general licenses authorizing transactions with the Palestinian Authority,
including OFAC General License No. 4 (issued April 4, 2006) and OFAC
General License No. 7 (issued June 20, 2007). General License No. 4
authorized U.S. persons to engage in all transactions with the Palestinian
Authority President and certain other entities, including PIF. General
License No. 7 includes the authorizations under previous licenses by
providing broad authorization for U.S. persons to engage in all
transactions with the Palestinian Authority otherwise prohibited by the
terrorism sanctions programs, noted above.

General License No. 7 does not authorize transactions with Hamas, a
U.S.-designated terrorist organization which is still a target of the
sanctions programs. Provisions in U.S. annual appropriations acts have
prohibited funding for Hamas or a Hamas-controlled entity and generally

---

[3]OFAC "targets" an individual, group, or entity by placing its name on a Specially
Designated Nationals (SDN) list. In addition to its country sanctions, OFAC publishes a list
of individuals and companies owned or controlled by, or acting on behalf of, targeted
countries, which may include senior government officials and persons who provide
substantial economic and political support for those governments. It also lists individuals,
groups, and entities, such as terrorists and narcotic traffickers designated under programs
that are not country specific. Collectively, such individuals and entities are called
"Specifically Designated Nationals and Blocked Persons" or "SDNs." Their assets are
blocked, and U.S. persons are generally prohibited from dealing with them.

[4]A license is an authorization from OFAC to engage in a transaction that otherwise would
be prohibited. There are two types of licenses: general licenses and specific licenses. A
general license authorizes a particular type of transaction for a class of persons without
the need to apply for a license. A specific license is a written document issued by OFAC to
a particular person or entity, authorizing a particular transaction in response to a written
license application.

prohibited funding for a power-sharing government of which Hamas is a member or that results from an agreement with Hamas and over which Hamas exercises undue influence, though under certain conditions, assistance may be provided to such a power-sharing government. See Consolidated Appropriations Act, 2010, Pub. L. No. 111-117, §7040(f), 123 Stat. 3034 at 3367-68, Dec. 16, 2009, and Consolidated Appropriations Act, 2012, Pub. L. No. 112-74, §7040(f), 125 Stat. 786 at 1222, Dec. 23, 2011.

USAID Policies and Procedures

The USAID Mission to the West Bank and Gaza developed USAID/West Bank and Gaza Mission Order 21[5] to implement E.O. 13224 and the vetting provisions in annual foreign operations appropriations legislation. The Mission's antiterrorism policies and procedures, as provided in revised Mission Order 21,[6] state that the Mission must vet certain non-U.S. recipients of USAID funding, which involves checking recipients' names and other identifying information against databases and other information sources to determine if they are involved with terrorism. In addition, the order clarifies how its antiterrorism policies and procedures apply to USAID assistance instruments, by requiring, among other things, that (1) all solicitations and awards for such assistance instruments contain an antiterrorism clause that reminds award recipients that they

[5]The Secretary of State deferred to USAID, the implementing agency, to ensure compliance with the vetting requirements in annual foreign operations appropriations legislation. In addition, State is currently working with USAID to set up a pilot program for a comprehensive partner vetting system as authorized by the Consolidated Appropriations Act, 2010, Pub. L. No. 111-117, § 7034(o), Dec. 16, 2009. The act restricts the use of funds by State or USAID to implement a partner vetting system, except that funds appropriated by the act may be used to implement a partner vetting system pilot program, to be applied equally to the programs and activities of State and USAID.

[6]Mission Order 21 was originally issued March 17, 2006, and revised and updated May 26, 2006, and October 3, 2007. See Mission Notice No. 2007-WBG-26. The Mission published implementing guidance in 2002 and 2003 concerning terrorist vetting and certification procedures (2002-West Bank and Gaza-05, Mar. 26, 2002; 2003-Dir.-01, Aug. 26, 2003). Mission Order 21 cites several legal authorities for its antiterrorism procedures. These include (1) E.O. 13224; (2) 18 U.S.C. §§ 2339A and 2339B; and (3) Executive Orders 12947 (Jan. 23, 1995) and 13099 (Aug. 20, 1998) which prohibit transactions with terrorists who threaten the Middle East peace process. Mission Order 21 also includes the antiterrorism vetting provisions of special relevance to the USAID Mission in the West Bank and Gaza in § 559 of the Foreign Operations Export Financing and Related Appropriations Act, 2006 (Pub. Law No. 109-102) and similar provisions in subsequent foreign operations appropriations acts, including § 7039(b) and (c) of the Consolidated Appropriations Act, 2012, Pub. L. No. 112-74, Dec. 23, 2011.

must comply with U.S. executive orders and laws prohibiting transactions with terrorists and the provision of resources and support to individuals or organizations associated with terrorism; (2) all U.S. and non-U.S. organizations sign an antiterrorism certification before being awarded a grant or cooperative agreement to certify that the organization does not provide material support or resources for terrorism; and (3) all assistance instruments contain a naming clause that states that no assistance shall be provided under the instrument for any school, community center, or other facility that is named after any person or group that has advocated, sponsored, or committed acts of terrorism.

USAID has also issued various policy directives since 2002 that implement Executive Order 13224 and applicable antiterrorism laws that require antiterrorism certification and antiterrorism clauses with respect to all awards. Among other things, those directives require USIAD personnel to check OFAC's SDGT list prior to making an award (see AAPD 02-04 [Mar. 20, 2002], ADS 302.3.5.5 and -.3.6.12 [Mar. 23, 2007], and PEB 2005-12 [July 20, 2006]); require all U.S. and non-U.S. organizations to certify, before being awarded a USAID grant or cooperative agreement, that the organization does not provide material support or resources for terrorism, (ADS 303 Jan. 30, 2007) and AAPD 04-14 (Sept. 24, 2004)[7]; and require inclusion of a mandatory clause in all solicitations and awards for contracts, grants, cooperative agreements, and subcontracts and subawards that reminds USAID contractors and implementing partners of their legal duty to comply with applicable antiterrorism laws (AAPD 02-04 and PEB 2005-12).[8]

---

[7]AAPD 04-14 superseded earlier versions of the directive issued in AAPD 02-19 (Dec. 31, 2002 and AAPD 04-07 (Mar. 24, 2004).

[8]In addition, on February 14, 2012, USAID issued a final rule amending its AIDAR regulations at 48 CFR Chapter 7 to implement a comprehensive Partner Vetting System (PVS) pilot program for USAID assistance and acquisition awards. See 77 Fed. Reg. 8166-8174, Feb. 14, 2012. The PVS pilot program was authorized by the Consolidated Appropriations Act, 2010, Pub. L. No. 111-117, § 7034(o), Dec. 16, 2009. That act restricts the use of funds by the State Department or USAID to implement a partner vetting system, except that funds appropriated by the act may be used to implement a partner vetting system pilot program, to be applied equally to the programs and activities of State and USAID. The Consolidated Appropriations Act, 2012, § 7034(i) directed State and USAID to implement the PVS pilot program no later than September 30, 2012.

OPIC Policies and Procedures

OPIC has developed "Security and Character Reference/Due Diligence (CRDD) Procedures, contained in the OPIC Operations Manual, which are intended to uncover any derogatory information—including risks for terrorist financing and money laundering—about projects in which OPIC is involved, the project sponsors, investors, and key personnel. According to OPIC's CRDD procedures, in performing CRDD for a project, a project team must make use of necessary information sources that may include (1) OPIC's Information Center databases; (2) the FBI's Terrorist Screening Center and Treasury's Financial Crimes Enforcement Network; (3) relevant U.S. Embassy, any local counsel, and when required, Outsourced Foreign Searches (OFS) Information Center; (4) State Department Bureau of Intelligence Research; and (5) OIP, with respect to derogatory information regarding social responsibility, corporate image, and environmental accountability.

OPIC's policies regarding loan guarantees and affordable mortgage programs relating to PIF and other entities in the West Bank and Gaza are based on the U.S. government security/ character vetting process, according to OPIC officials.

Appendix IV: GAO Contact and Staff Acknowledgments

GAO Contact	David Gootnick, (202) 512-3149 or gootnickd@gao.gov
Staff Acknowledgments	In addition to the individual named above, Godwin Agbara (Assistant Director), Barbara Shields, Martin De Alteriis, Karen Deans, Etana Finkler, Ernie Jackson, and Nicholas Jepson made key contributions to this report. Other contributors include Shirley Brothwell, Brian Egger, Kay Halpern, Mathew Scire, and Steven Westley.

Related GAO Products

Foreign Assistance: U.S. Assistance to the West Bank and Gaza for Fiscal Years 2010 and 2011. GAO-12-817R. Washington, D.C.: July 13, 2012.

Foreign Assistance: U.S. Assistance to the West Bank and Gaza for Fiscal Years 2008 and 2009. GAO-10-623R. Washington, D.C.: May 14, 2010.

Foreign Assistance: Measures to Prevent Inadvertent Payments to Terrorists under Palestinian Aid Programs Have Been Strengthened, but Some Weaknesses Remain. GAO-09-622. Washington, D.C.: May 19, 2009.

Foreign Assistance: Recent Improvements Made, but USAID Should Do More to Help Ensure Aid Is Not Provided for Terrorist Activities in West Bank and Gaza. GAO-06-1062R. Washington, D.C.: September 29, 2006.

Foreign Assistance: Middle East Partnership Initiative Offers Tool for Supporting Reform, but Project Monitoring Needs Improvement. GAO-05-711. Washington, D.C.: August 8, 2005.